Facebook Marketing Guide

The Distilled Step-by-Step Guide to Facebook Marketing, Advertising and Community Building

By Jeff Abston

Table of Contents

Introduction

With over 1.8 billion in monthly active users, it's very clear that Facebook isn't slowing down anytime soon. Facebook has been proven to be a platform that any business, brand or company can only ignore at their peril, especially if they intend to have a share of the social media marketing platform. With an ocean of potential customers on the platform that one can successfully reach, it takes effort for a business to stand out and get a worthy market share.

With such a large audience pool out there, many businesses are competing for space; it takes a unique Facebook marketing strategy to realize a worthwhile return on investment. Many people have failed to realize tangible results with their Facebook marketing campaigns due to a lack of proper understanding of the platform and how best to go through the marketing process. **Facebook Marketing** delves deeper into what marketing on Facebook entails.

The book covers in detail various marketing strategies that, if taken into account and carefully implemented, have the potential of transforming one's business with great results. Many business owners have found huge successes with Facebook marketing; by learning and implementing their strategies, you will get a good grasp of how Facebook algorithms can yield great results. Facebook marketing can be a success if one has clear goals that match their needs. Structuring a marketing strategy to address these goals and objectives can have a big impact by influencing both reach and conversion rate.

Whether you intend to use Facebook for marketing or are just looking for ways to revamp your marketing strategies, you will get valuable information in this book. The way you carry out every step of the process right from creating a Facebook page, organizing your about page and establishing the settings is critical. As much as gaining organic reach is great, you may also need to invest more effort by engaging in paid marketing. The fact that you engage in paid marketing doesn't guarantee great results, especially if the steps are not well executed. Ensure that you don't create unrealistic goals with vanity metrics such as gaining more likes and followers; instead, you should rise above this and address your bigger challenges.

By addressing the challenges effectively, you will be able to realize great returns. Understanding the marketing strategies and implementing them effectively will definitely result in increased sales, enhanced brand visibility and awareness, and even steady business growth. Facebook is always revising their app and having a good understanding of the platform will enable you to get the most out of the newly-introduced updates that may give you an edge over the competition. Demographics are normally vital for any marketing strategy, so taking time to study the insights to understand your audience better can yield great results.

Take your time to read the book all the way through to the end; you never know which strategy could be vital in pushing your brand forward.

Chapter 1: Understanding Facebook Marketing

Facebook is one of the largest social network platforms in the world with at least more than 1.30 billion active users, meaning that about 62% of users log into Facebook daily, a fact that makes it such a dynamic marketing platform. According to eMarketer, about 41% of US small businesses use Facebook as part of their online marketing strategy. The momentum with which Facebook has grown right from its launch a few years ago to where it is today only shows that it will likely experience continual growth in the future. Having such a large user base makes it a great selling platform, and ignoring it isn't an option for serious marketers.

Even with the widespread use of Facebook for marketing purposes, only about 45% of business owners have reported success with their Facebook marketing efforts, according to a survey carried out by Social Media Examiner. Business owners therefore need to understand the strategies and practices capable of granting them a positive return on investment that's worth the effort. Understanding the major components of Facebook marketing is vital to equip business owners with best practices and actionable insights that, if properly implemented, have the potential of giving the desired results.

Every day, Facebook presents entrepreneurs with a market for their products and services, and the question arises as to how one can target such a huge user base. Facebook has made it easy for marketers to establish an advertising platform and specify the type of people they want to target with their strategies. Marketers can target the right market using location of users, as well as interests and demographics. Understanding how you can use Facebook marketing to your advantage is quite vital for the success of a business.

Facebook started as a social network platform for college students, but has so far evolved into a platform that anyone with an Internet connection can access. The minimum age required for users is just 13 years, which covers a wide base of users, and it is being used by people of all ages. Facebook is popularly used by those between 18 and 65; however, the above and below age groups tend to minimally engage with the platform. Regardless of the age group you're targeting, you will find more than enough users to interact with on Facebook.

Engaging in Facebook marketing can help you realize may things:

- Strengthen brand identity
- Collect feedback from customers and build customer relationships
- Direct customers to your website
- Ability to be found by those looking for your products
- Create targeted advertising for promoting your business
- Generate word of mouth advertising
- Establish and demonstrate your expertise

How to Market on Facebook

There are three tools that marketers can use for marketing on Facebook. These tools are Facebook pages, Facebook ads and Facebook Groups. Each of the tools has a way to be used and often varies; however, all can be used together for greater reach of the targeted market.

Pages

Facebook page is similar to a profile; however, it's mostly used by organizations, businesses and public figures. Users get to "like" the page which then automatically enables them to receive updates from it into their newsfeeds. Unlike profiles that require mutual friendships, pages can be liked by anybody. Pages also don't have any restriction on the number of people who can like the page unlike profiles that are limited to 5,000 people. Pages are quite easy to set up; bu7t building a fun base or a team of committed customers can be quite a challenge.

Ads

This is a targeted advertising platform marketers can use to create ads that target specific geographic areas; they can be filtered in terms of education levels, age and the type of devices used for browsing. Users are free to close ads they don't like and can "like" the page just below the advertisement. Ads are designed with powerful parameters that are quite ideal for targeting: the only downside is that they can be a bit expensive depending on one's goal.

Groups

Facebook groups are akin to discussion forums but have additional features similar to profiles and pages. You can create a group related to your area of business or industry, enabling you to connect with potential customers. Groups are free to use and allow for high levels of engagement. The challenge is that they can be quite time consuming.

There are various marketing strategies that can be used on Facebook; however, focusing on what is less expensive has the potential of bringing greater returns and is thus quite beneficial for business purposes. Inbound marketing is one of the ways that tends to yield great returns if well executed. It entails engaging with your audience in a way they find relatable and helpful. It involves getting to know customer goals and collaborating with them as you help them overcome the challenges they face. The best way to execute this strategy is by being available where your audience spends time - which is Facebook.

The tools available for marketers on Facebook cater to those willing to form relationships with their audience. Marketers should be able to create and distribute content that their audience finds valuable and helpful. Quality content enables marketers to connect with consumers interested in the services offered or their brands. Pushing content that your audience is not interested in can be perceived as annoying, spammy or even deceiving. Facebook marketing requires a long-term commitment and consistency in delivering quality content.

To succeed in Facebook marketing, one should clearly distinguish between Facebook advertising and Facebook marketing. As much as your Facebook marketing strategy may incorporate Facebook advertising, your strategy should also involve building engaging and lasting relationships with your audience. The content you share should not always be geared towards making a sale or pitching a product; connecting and providing helpful information to your social network can go a long way toward providing long-term reliable customers you can engage with.

You don't need a big budget to get started and be successful at Facebook marketing; commitment to providing valuable content in a reliable and consistent way can greatly help in connecting with potential customers and fans. All you have to do as you start out is to ensure that you highlight your brand values in a clear and effective way, identify your audience and their demographics, while also creating a unique space for your company. Remember that when it comes to Facebook marketing, sometimes the simplest form of communication can be the most powerful.

If you have a product or service that's considered to be boring, you can awe your audience by incorporating beautiful images to highlight the creative side of your brand. Take advantage of the virtual reality features provided on Facebook to enhance your content.

Developing a Facebook Marketing Strategy

Starting off with your Facebook marketing plan without having a clear strategy in place can only lead to failure, as you're likely to become overwhelmed in the process. Take time and define your marketing strategy; just going ahead and starting a Facebook page without a clear strategy may not grant you the desired results. You should have a clear strategy on how to meet your business goals and get the most out of every investment you make on Facebook. Below are some of the strategies you can consider putting in place.

Define your Audience

Targeting the right audience effectively may not be possible if you don't know your audience well. Defining it may not be easy if you're just starting out; however, an overview of Facebook demographics and having brand intelligence about the customer profile will act as the first building block in developing an understanding of how your audience may turn out to be. You can use tools such as Facebook audience insights to investigate key details about potential customers you may find on Facebook. Details such as age, gender, relationship status, education, location, Facebook usage and past purchase activity can give you insight into how to define your audience.

Set your Goals

Having clear marketing goals is also vital. You can invest in getting more "likes" to your business page; but if the likes are not part of your broader marketing plan, then having more likes may not yield great returns. Remember the goals differ from one business to another but should be based on specific actions that will have an impact on the bottom line, actions that lead to increased conversions to your website, generating leads and improving customer service response. These may be broad marketing goals, and you can consider goals that are more specific and measurable.

Every engagement you involve yourself in, whether it is posting content, making a comment or even designing an ad, should support your business goals. You can instill all the aspects of your Facebook marketing plan by having a marketing mission statement that suits your brand. It should enable you to maintain a brand voice that is consistent in all your Facebook marketing activities.

Having a goal gives the marketing process direction and is a way of measuring the success. Some of the business goals for using Facebook include:

- Find people searching for the services or products you are offering
- Connect and engage with potential and current customers
- Build a community around your business
- Promote your other content such as webinars, blog articles and the like

Create a Facebook Marketing Plan

Once you have set goals, you will then develop a clear plan on how to achieve them. One vital plan you should formulate is determining the ideal content mix for your audience. You can follow the common 80 – 20 rule. This is where 80 percent of your Facebook posts are focused on informing, educating and entertaining with the other 20 percent focused on directly promoting your brand. The key thing about Facebook you need to remember is that the engagements should be geared towards relationships, and the constant pitching of your products may not be the best way to build them.

If you're committed to providing valuable content that your followers find helpful and keeps them engaged, they will be open learning about the services or products you are offering with the 20 percent of the sales-focused posts. You can also follow the social media rule of thirds to provide a mix of promotional posts and valuable content. It entails a third of your content covering ideas and stories, a third involving personal interactions with your followers, and the remaining one-third focused on promoting your business. Regardless of the plan you choose, it should be aimed at providing more valuable content than promotional material so as to keep your audience engaged and interested.

According to Facebook algorithms, brands that focus more on driving sales often get penalized. Facebook require that users' feeds be filled with content they like and are willing to share instead of sales pitches. Remember that likes and shares help extend your reach as they puts your brand before many people without any direct effort from your side.

After defining your content mix, the next step is to determine how frequently you should post. As much as posts don't appear in their chronological order based on the algorithms, you can plan on posting at a time when your audience is more active on the platform. Establish a content calendar to help with balancing and mixing different types of content for your posting to be on track.

Chapter 2: Getting Started with Facebook Marketing

To get started with Facebook marketing, you need to begin by creating a business page. Your Facebook page is like your store or business presence on Facebook. It's also your online identity that expresses how your brand should be perceived. The Facebook page is the place where you get to post your content and engage with followers. It's free to create a Facebook page; however, it's important to keep some Facebook best practices in mind as you design it. To create a business page, you will need to have a personal profile account.

A personal profile account is meant for individuals while a page is meant for business purposes. Pages are designed with functionalities that make engaging in business tasks much easier, so you should avoid creating a personal profile for business purposes. Below are some factors you should put in place as you design your business page:

- Choose a business name that's search friendly - most likely your brand name.
- Set a custom URL for your business page. It should be consistent with your handle across different platforms.
- Ensure that you give sufficient information in your "about" section. Provide vital information regarding the business and details on how your followers can connect with you.
- Remember that your profile and cover photos create that first visual impression for your Facebook audience so you should ensure that it accurately represent your brand while

also encouraging potential followers to like and engage with the content and information you share.

- Remember to add a call-to-action button to make it easy for potential users to get in touch and connect with you or even to purchase your products.

To open a Facebook business account you need to first begin by signing up with Facebook. Go to www.facebook.com and open a personal Facebook account.

Once you have signed up for a personal account, go ahead and edit your profile at the right hand of the navigation bar. Add basic personal information as required such as birthday, relationship status, hometown, interests and About Me description. You can also add contact information and your education and work information. You can then go ahead and find out some important networks you may want to join. Joining a network can enable people to find you and also improves your ranking in a Facebook search.

Once your personal account is set up, the next step is to connect with friends, family, coworkers and other connections. You can use tools such as "Find Friends" to help you choose friends to connect with. You can also import your contact list and let Facebook search your email address book for people within your network. You can also see Facebook friend suggestions. Once you come across someone you know, just click "Add as Friend." Friends should be mutually accepted.

The next step with your personal account should be sharing information. You can share all kinds of information with your network such as videos, photos, notes, links and any relevant information. When you log onto your Facebook page, you will find a box that shows where you can type in information.

Any content you type will be featured on your wall tab and on your friends Newsfeeds. There are various applications that help you make your Facebook engagements more interactive. Some of the popular applications include events, movies, causes and photos. Remember that social media is all about building and establishing relationships, which can either be personal, business or any other, so it's vital that one stay authentic when using social media for business purposes.

People prefer connecting with real people and not faceless brands, and it's the personal connections that lead to business through word of mouth marketing or even referrals. If you feel uncomfortable with exposing your personal information, then you can customize your privacy settings to control who gets to see portions of your profile. Facebook also recommends the settings you can use, depending on who views your profile.

Facebook Business Page

A business page is more like a personal profile with the difference being that it's public and users can "like" your page and even become a fan without getting approval from the page admin. It's free to create a page but you will need sufficient time to build and maintain it. Even as you create your business page, remember that it's the first point for all your Facebook marketing efforts. You need a page capable of ranking in both Google and Facebook searches for your given brand name so that you can be easily located by both your customers and prospects.

Once your page is found by prospects and customers, it should be something that's appealing and worth spending time in. When they find the page to be appealing, they will likely choose to like or follow the page. You should therefore incorporate some best practices that will help optimize your page for better ranking. To create a page, log into your Facebook profile, then create your page. To create a page you can also visit www.facebook.com/pages/create/.

You will find six different page categories from which to choose:

- Local business or place
- Company, Organization or Institution
- Brand or Product
- Artist, Band or Public Figure
- Entertainment
- Cause or Community

Create a Page

Give your brand, business or cause a voice on Facebook and connect with the people who matter to you. It's free to set up. Just choose a Page type to get started.

Local business or place	Company, Organisation or Institution	Brand or product
Artist, Band or Public Figure	Entertainment	Cause or Community

Select Appropriate Category for your Business

It's quite possible to set up a category that's not right for your business, which can create a serious problem especially if you intend to show up in Facebook Graph Search. If your business is a local one, then just go ahead and select the category as your business type as it will enable people to check in at your local business place. If you don't have any need for walk-ins to your business, you can opt for the companies and organizations category as it would be more appropriate. Choose the category that's ideal for your business, then go ahead and start creating the page. Regardless of the option you choose, you will have to customize the about fields to suit your type of business.

You need to choose the name for your business wisely as changing the name later can be quite tedious.

Optimize Page Images

Your cover photo and profile pictures are the first visual impressions that visitors get the moment they visit your page. To give your Facebook page identity a professional look, you should choose images with a professional flair. These images should reflect the desired look and feel of your brand or what you intend to create. Ensure they meet the required optimal size so as not to appear skewed. The profile picture you choose will appear on search results alongside any content you share, so this should be taken into consideration.

As you select the right profile picture, ensure that you choose the right dimensions for the photo; they should be square like 180px x 180px. Choose something recognizable for a business profile like a logo; or if you're a public speaker, then opt for an ideal headshot. Once you have chosen a profile photo, go ahead and choose a cover photo for your Facebook page. The dimensions for a cover photo should be 851 x 316 pixels. If your photo is not of these exact dimensions, you can drag and reposition it before saving. You can change the cover photo anytime by hovering over the white camera on the profile photo.

Choose a Memorable and Descriptive Username

As you create your page, ensure every step is optimized for SEO and likes as that's what will enhance your marketing strategy. Your Facebook username is more like a web address for your page. Your page will automatically get a default URL, which may even include numbers. This is why you need to choose a username that conveys your ideal business accurately. A good username will convey the right information about your business so that customers and prospects can easily find you on Google and Facebook search platforms. Remember that you must have at least 25 likes to claim a vanity URL. Keep your page's unique URL handy as you will need it when you begin to promote your page, your blog or other engagements that can grant you more likes. Once you are through with these steps, you can add shortcuts that will grant you easy access to your page. To crate shortcuts, go to the Newsfeed, then click on edit which is next to shortcuts.

Use Descriptive Keywords for Your About Section

Once you have created the cover photo, and have chosen a URL, you can go ahead and add a description for your page. You can click "About", then go ahead and fill in all the necessary information about your business. The About section is like text-based real estate of your page. Ensure that you describe your business accurately alongside your products or services by using the keywords that customers are likely to employ in their search queries. Remember to include your website URL in the description as well to encourage clicks to your website.

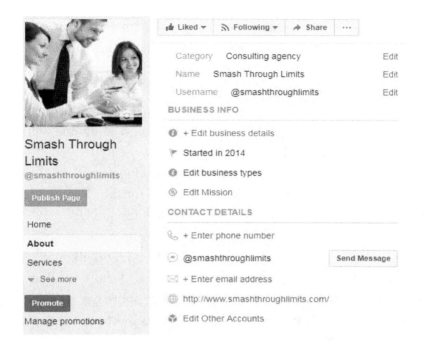

Set up Roles

Once you are through with these basic steps, you can go ahead and set up roles. One great thing about a Facebook page is the fact that multiple numbers of people can make edits on the page unlike a personal profile; that can be done without having to share the login credentials. You, therefore, have to designate the level of access for whomever you choose - that's what page role entails. On the top navigation bar, you click on Settings; then as you look down under settings, you will see page roles in the left navigation bar. There are various roles you can assign people:

Assign a New Page Role

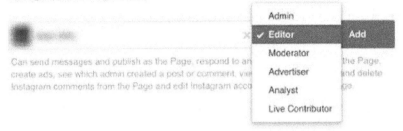

Admins: Admins have the authority to manage all aspects of the page, which means they can send messages, respond to messages, delete comments, create ads, publish the page and even see the admin who published a given post or even assigned page roles. An admin has similar permission as the creator of the page. You should, therefore, be careful when choosing admins.

Editor: They have similar roles as the admins with the only difference being the inability to assign page roles.

Moderator: They can send messages and even respond to or delete comments, but they can't publish the page. They do have access to create ads.

Advertiser: Can create ads and view page insights.

Analyst: They don't have the authority to publish but can see posts published by admins and can also view insights.

Live contributor: They can go live on their mobile to the page, but they are not authorized to comment, view insights, create ads or even have access to publishing tools. Below is the window for assigning a new page role.

While still under Settings, you can customize how you want to receive alerts for page activity. You can do this by going to

Notifications and selecting to receive an alert every time there's an activity on your page or after a given time.

Add a Facebook CTA

One thing that makes a Facebook page ideal for a business is the ability to attract a unique audience that you may not have attracted before or even reached through a website. However, it's important to know that a buyer's journey may not end on Facebook. Facebook pages now have a call-to-action button which makes it possible to engage with an audience and share what you want them to do, whether it's booking your service, making a purchase, or even getting in touch. There is an array of choices that you can choose from. You can choose a link for the CTA, where you can direct your customers to such as your home page, a video or your landing page.

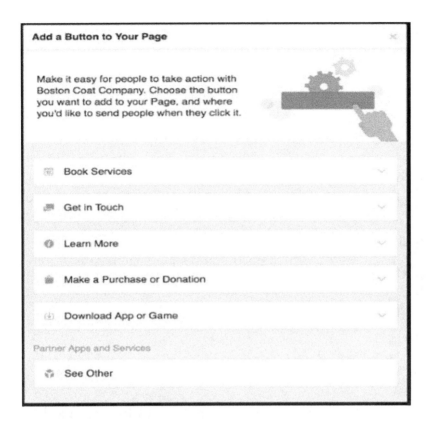

Add a Button to Your Page   ✕

Make it easy for people to take action with
Boston Coat Company. Choose the button
you want to add to your Page, and where
you'd like to send people when they click it.

🗐   Book Services   ⌄

🗇   Get In Touch   ⌄

⊕   Learn More   ⌄

🛒   Make a Purchase or Donation   ⌄

⊕   Download App or Game   ⌄

Partner Apps and Services

🕸   See Other

To take your Facebook business page to the next level, you should
then add custom tabs so as to tailor the content that users get to
view whenever they visit your page. For example, a visit to the
Starbucks page gives you various options for what you intend to
browse. You can choose to browse photos, visit Pinterest, and
check out open jobs and the like.

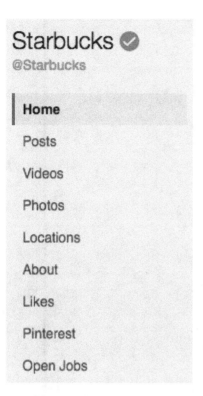

Starbucks ✓
@Starbucks

Home

Posts

Videos

Photos

Locations

About

Likes

Pinterest

Open Jobs

To change your page tabs, go to Manage Tabs towards the left navigation. Then you can choose from the pre-made options. You can go ahead and verify your business page and by going to settings, then clicking on page verification, and following the details. Verifying your page may not be necessary, but it gives your page a sense of authority. It may be ideal for businesses that offer online services or those in an ecommerce business. Verifying your account may lead to establishing trust with potential customers and you will be able to initiate some transactions online.

How to get Facebook Likes and Fans

As much as your goal is to realize success in your business, your success on the platform will mostly be determined by your goals, so your focus and priority should be to launch new products, create awareness, collect leads to your website and drive sales. You should therefore focus on getting as many likes and fans as possible. A "like" simply means that someone is interested in getting updates from your business in their newsfeed. As much as many people invest in buying Facebook likes, since it seems the fastest way to make your business look more credible, it's not the best way to get them for your Facebook page.

Most companies that sell Facebook likes often use fake or compromised accounts to realize the numbers. It means that the users found in such a way may never engage with your content. Remember that not all the posts you make show up on the newsfeed, Facebook decides on the posts to include, depending on the engagement rates. So a lack of engagement with your content in terms of comments and likes in comparison to page likes may prevent your page from being seen. An average user may look at the level of engagement and question your credibility.

Start Posting

Now that your Facebook page is ready, the next step is to make a post. You can either create a text post or a photo to create awareness about your page and spark engagement within Facebook. Even as you post texts, it's advisable that you add a photo as it helps boost the number of likes and comments you get. If you're unsure where to get relevant photos, check out the numerous free stock photo sites available online. You should be well conversant with image copyright issues before sharing any photo you come across.

You shouldn't restrict yourself to a photo; you can consider other images such as info graphics, an illustration, or any other visual content that can help enhance engagement with your content. Even sharing an image like the one below can help create interest with your text.

Facebook Video Post

Many users find video content to be quite compelling and posting video content can create a strong visual appeal for your product. If you are looking for ways to tell a compelling story that's more engaging, then you should consider posting video content. Facebook Videos generally start to play automatically over the viewer's newsfeed, a fact that makes it catch anyone's eye, even if it runs for just a minute. Posting a video can therefore have a great impact and enhance engagement with your content, even if it runs for a few seconds. Longer video posts have also proven to be highly shareable content across social media platforms, and they can attract thousands or even millions of views. Video connect is therefore an ideal way of connecting with followers.

The video content you share should be accessible, easy to digest and have captions. The videos you create should have the potential of catching the user attention, providing them with valuable information.

Facebook Live Video

Facebook live video is also a great way of sharing content and engaging with your followers. It has been proven to drive engagements three times over. It's another option you can use to explore more multimedia content. Facebook allows for live streaming capabilities. It's a nice way of giving them access to a behind-the-scenes outlook of your company and your products, and maybe some of the personalities involved with your brand. Facebook live videos enable you to share real-time announcements that are ideal for your business and your Facebook followers as well.

As in-the-moment content continues to soar in popularity, you should figure out how your brand can provide a sneak peak of the industry, product launches, or office events by going live. As you engage in Facebook live, just know that anything can happen in the process, so you need to be well prepared in advance.

Linked Content Post

This entails linking content outside Facebook to your Facebook page. It could be content on your blog or website. All you have to do when linking content to your Facebook is to copy and paste the link to your Facebook status box. It will then pull the photo and the content's meta description to the page. You will get a great post with very little effort and all you need to do is to add some text to inform readers why they should click on the link. As much as you will be sharing most of your content, you can also share those of leaders who your followers may find valuable.

To figure out the type of content to post, you need to engage more in social listening. Look out for information regarding what potential customers, fans and competitors are posting online, then provide some insight that they should find extremely valuable. Look out for what existing customers love about your business or products, the challenges that people have of which you are well aware that your business can address and how you can differentiate yourself and stand out from the competition. Engaging in social listening can help you in answering such questions through your Facebook posts.

You can also check out if any of your content has received a great response, so you can share that content on Facebook. You should have a page on your blog that's always getting new comments.

Pinned Post

Various research studies and experiences have proven that most people will visit your page only once and either "like" the page or just leave. If they like your page, then they will go on to interact with the content that appears in their newsfeed; but most will hardly visit your wall again. So the primary purpose of your page should be geared towards getting people to like your page. Facebook authorizes page admins to pin one post at the top of the page. This is a post that you pin at the top of your Facebook page so that it's not driven down whenever you post new content.

It's that one piece of content that soars above the rest and captures your brand, while also showing potential followers why they should "like" your page and engages with your content. Ensure that the topic of the post is interesting, unique and has an image that's eye-catching

Schedule Facebook Content through your Social Media Calendar

If you are to see consistent engagement, then you need a clear schedule for posting your content. If you fail to schedule, you might find yourself posting hastily and even skipping it when you don't have sufficient time. Such a move can have quite a negative impact on your marketing strategy. Planning your content enables you to put greater focus on the quality of your content, making it possible to engage with your audience effectively and even inspiring them as desired.

Since you may not always have the time to create content, you can take advantage of some of the available publishing tools. When you opt to use publishing tools, you will only be left to monitor and maintain your account to ensure the content quality is good and that you have posted according to the planned schedule. Remember that when it comes to Facebook marketing, growing brand loyalty takes effort and time, so you should be committed to the tried and true strategies if you are to realize tangible results.

Chapter 3: Promoting Your Facebook Business Page

One of the ways you can use to promote your business is to encourage social sharing by using Facebook plugins and buttons. Your Facebook page and website need to work seamlessly together, and your marketing funnel should effectively work at directing traffic to your website. You should provide a way for your visitors to share your content and also interact with your page. Each piece of content you share on your page should have a "like" and "share" button for easy sharing and engagement. To make it easy for followers to interact with your page, you can install a page plugin on your website sidebar. You can customize your posts in a way that shows a preview of page posts for enhanced engagements.

Getting Your Posts Seen by More Fans

If there is one thing that fuels online marketing, then its traffic, the more traffic you get to your business page, the more success you're likely to realize. Without traffic, making headway in the online business space can be quite a challenge. The good thing is that most businesses have proved that a huge number of their customers and referrals come from social media platforms, with Facebook the dominant one. You will not just get business by posting content and leaving your Facebook page, but you also need to look for ways to promote your business on Facebook to get more followers and likes.

There are two ways to promote your Facebook page and - organic or the paid promotion. As you consider engaging in promoting your Facebook page, remember that Facebook provides users with valuable content only, so in order to increase the user engagement, you need to optimize the user experience with content tailored to the user's experience. Engaging in strategies that result in organic reach can be of great benefit as they help in nurturing leads and fostering organic conversion, among other benefits.

Attracting potential buyers organically can be great as you get to engage with them and convert them to your sales funnel at virtually no cost apart from the time and effort you invest. The cost of converting potential buyers into customers will be much less; so the more organic reach you can get, the better will be your lead generation and conversion process. If your Facebook marketing strategy is to be effective, you have to understand the Facebook newsfeed algorithm. Understanding the Facebook algorithm helps you to make sense of the numerous pieces of contents being shared daily by businesses and how they choose the posts that get featured in the newsfeed.

Facebook Algorithm Values

Understanding algorithms begins by understanding the core values that influence the way they work. Knowing this provides a hint on posts that will do well and those that may not on Facebook. According to Facebook values; the following should be taken into account.

Friends and family are given priority: The main objective of the Facebook newsfeed is to connect people with their friends and family. Their posts will always be given priority. After featuring posts from family and friends, Facebook then gives priority to those that inform and entertain users.

Platform for all ideas: Facebook as a platform welcomes all manner of ideas but ensures that everyone is safe. They focus on delivering information that each individual desires to see according to their actions on the platform and feedback given.

Authentic communications: Facebook gives priority to stories that are genuine instead of misleading, spammy and sensational ones.

You control your experience: Facebook gives users the opportunity to customize their Facebook experience because individuals know what's best for them. Users have the choice to unfollow or even see preferred content.

Constant Iteration: Facebook is ever collecting feedback that helps improve the platform operation.

Below are some of the factors that influence the Facebook algorithm:

- Preference is given to posts with many likes, shares and comments.
- Posts that within a short time get a high volume of comments, likes and shares.
- Linked posts
- Posts commented on, liked or shared by a friend
- Posts that one interacts frequently with
- Posts that users tend to prefer such as status updates, photos and videos.
- Shared videos that receive higher views with an extended viewing duration
- Posts that reference a trending topic or that are timely
- Posts from pages where fan bases overlap with a fan base of other pages of high quality.

The Facebook algorithm doesn't give priority to the following posts:

- Click bait, like baiting and posts with spammy links
- Repeated posts and frequently circulated content
- Text only updates from pages
- Posts of low quality that are frequently hidden
- Posts that ask people for likes, comments or shares
- Posts with unusual engagement patterns like a baiting signal
- Contents that are overly promotional that push people to buy a product or a service, those that encourage people to enter into a contest, and those that reuse the same text extracted from ads.

Create a Facebook Group

As much as you have a Facebook business page, it's important that you also add a Facebook group to your marketing strategy. Using Facebook groups helps in enhancing engagement with your target market. When groups are used correctly, they can act as a great source of traffic, which may then lead to increased engagement with prospective customers. Groups provide a platform where you get to share information and ideas with users who are like minded. You can also establish authority in your given field by participating in other people's industry-related groups.

Engaging with groups by offering valuable advice and tips can make others consider you as a valued member of the group and people will get to trust you more. Once they recognize how valuable you are to the group, they will then engage with you and even trust you more. Participating in Facebook groups can be beneficial if you get to either create or participate in groups related to your interest. Groups give one the opportunity to engage with their audience in a way that's quite personal and relatable.

You also get to be involved in your target market's day-to-day conversations. You can create a group that encourages conversation on anything related to your industry. Creating your own Facebook group provides an effective way to gather followers and fans in one place, where you can encourage them to interact with one another to build an active community of people who are talking and sharing information about your business. A group also provides a platform where you can gather customer intelligence regarding what people are saying about your business. It's more like a focus group with unlimited members and a place where you can dive into and facilitate a conversation or even ask questions.

Facebook groups provide a great way to showcase your knowledge and experience to your audience while you also build important connections with the most engaged users. Remember that the group doesn't have to be big, so to create a lot of engagement, you should make the group interactive even with a smaller number. In some instances your fans can create a group that focuses on our brand. The best thing to do is to join groups just to ensure that the conversation going on is factual and positive.

Below are some of the strategies you can engage in to promote your Facebook page:

Automate everything

Remember that Facebook is a social media platform, so your brand should actually have that human touch. Instead of just posting links to your latest blogs and your product updates, you can also post team photos or something creative and funny that shows your human nature. For example, a photo like the one below by the o-Business team can greatly enhance the human connection when shared with content. You can also share some interesting graphics for enhanced optimization.

Promote your products and services only

Facebook is generally based on user interest and not intent, so ensure that you don't always send promotional updates. Remember that 80% of your posts should be social; otherwise users will get irritated and may click the "unlike" button. Try to approach your Facebook page with the attitude of building a community and focus on adding value to the conversation and engagements you get involved in with your audience. The content you share should express the following:

- Brand story posts
- Authority building posts
- Lead nurture posts
- Personal posts

Avoid building a Fan Base you Cannot Sustain

One challenge of a wider fan base is the fact that regardless of how targeted it may be, your reach may still be quite low. Having a large fan base requires that you put a lot of effort in creating content that the different segments of your followers will find useful. It's better to have a smaller but highly engaged audience instead of a larger and unresponsive one.

How to track and analyze your organic reach

Now that you are more aware of what to do and not to do, you can now take time to analyze your organic reach so that you can work to improve it. You need to gather metrics that show you where the shortcomings are and areas you can improve on for enhanced organic reach. Without carrying out this type of diagnosis, you may not have a clear understanding of where you should be concentrating your efforts. Below are some of the things you need to do to track and analyze your organic reach.

Export Insights data From Your Facebook Page

Once you click on insights, you will find a button that enables you to export data for both posts and page engagements. A window will then pop up with options for your insights. You can then select "export data" and the data will be saved into an Excel file.

Take Time to Analyze the Post Metrics

Post level metrics are generally more insightful then page metrics. While page metrics give you an overall view of your performance, post metrics give a more detailed view on how users interact with your content. That's what makes all the difference. You can then use the data you get to ascertain the posts with the highest organic reach, those that the audience preferred and the number of likes you got on each post. You can use the information to launch a more effective content strategy.

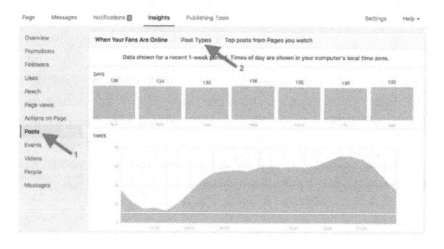

Fine Tune the Data by Selecting the Metrics you Need

You can fine tune your data by looking at the organic reach, the level of engagement with the posts, the link clicks and the number of users who gave negative feedback. Once you have analyzed your data and know the strategies to take, you can formulate ways to improve your organic search.

Chapter 4: Ways to enhance Facebook Organic Reach

A Facebook marketing strategy can be carried out in two dominant ways: either by engaging in paid marketing or engaging in activities that enhance organic reach. This chapter will mainly focus on Facebook marketing through enhanced organic reach. If you don't have the dollars to spend on advertising, then engaging in organic marketing strategies can equally yield great results. However, you will need to put more effort and time in implementing these strategies. There are various strategies you can use to enhance your organic reach, and this is one of the ways to grow your audience with minimal effort.

Paid ads can be quite costly, especially if you are starting out. Below are some of the strategies you can engage in for enhanced Facebook organic reach:

Build your Brand Presence and Authority

Growing your brand presence may not necessarily be about increasing page "likes" as the number of likes may not give a clear indication of how the content will perform. Building a brand presence means cultivating a sense of authority that moves your audience to take action, getting them to engage favorably with your content. To grow your brand presence and authority, you need to engage in the following:

Attract the right people to your Facebook page: Attracting random fans may not add much value to your marketing strategy, as they hardly engage with your content and lack any form of positive influence on it. You need to attract people who are interested in your business ideals and willing to engage with the content you share on Facebook. Since they'll find the content relevant, it will show in their newsfeeds.

To attract a targeted audience, you need a strong brand presence. Remember that if your brand isn't that solid, then your audience too may not be. You need a brand image that stick in their minds and hearts. Remember, be consistent with posting content relevant to your audience and your business too. You can also use the audience insights to create a target persona for Facebook. Look out for the pain points, the interests of your target audience, their attitudes towards your industry or business and the objections they may have and how you intend to address them.

Once you have identified the persona, go ahead and target that demographic through your posts. As you boost your content, look out for those who have liked your content but not your page, and go ahead and invite them to "like" your page. Another way of targeting the right audience is by adding integrations and customizations to your page as shared earlier. You can also cross promote your other social media platforms such as Twitter, Pinterest, LinkedIn and others with Facebook. If you have a sizable following on any of these platforms, you can make use of them for growing your Facebook page.

Publish Evergreen Content Regularly

To enhance your Facebook organic reach, you will need to post evergreen content regularly. Whether your goal for the Facebook page is to generate traffic to your website or generate revenue, posting fresh content is one of the most powerful tools available. It's not only Google that considers freshness of content in their ranking, but the life of any content on the Facebook newsfeed also depends on how evergreen and recent the content is. If you keep posting content that's timeless, then your audience will find it useful for a longer period of time. The durability of posts can be boosted by posting evergreen content that can stay for hours and still engage your audience.

You can also repurpose the posts that are performing well to ensure that you get maximum reach from them. You can do this by changing text content to video content. You can tweak the post a little bit for a fresh feeling then repost. You can go ahead and curate other people's evergreen content. Examples of evergreen content and curated type posts are: video tutorials, testimonials, interviews, how to posts, thought pieces, lists and the like. To ensure that your fans get your posts, you can encourage them to go to your Facebook page and click on Get Notifications. They will then be able to get notifications for all your Facebook updates. This strategy can only work well if your relationship with your fans is a great one.

Create Invite Only Groups for the Most Engaged Audience Members

Facebook is all about building communities, and having a tightly knit group can be great for enhanced connections. Most people prefer groups for their brands and businesses, their products or services, a given lifestyle such as journaling or a book, and specific topics such as content marketing. The most valuable groups are either brand specific or even product specific. You can use a brand specific group to nurture a community around your business; it's a great marketing tool for the products or services you are offering.

A product or service specific group should be more focused on customer loyalty and retention. Once you have created the group, remember that it's your duty to sensitize people to join. Most people will want to join because of the community support. As new members join the group, you should ignite conversations relevant to your given industry that help in boosting engagement. Avoid solely promoting or selling your products and services. Some of the ways to increase engagement include: giving active members of the group admin or publisher status as they can assist in nurturing the group.

You can also carry out live Q&A's and consider creating challenges for the group. Ensure that you also have a content strategy; this you can do by creating content themes, then inciting some user-generated content campaigns. The user-generated content campaigns normally drive higher engagement which is more than brand-generated content. This is an example of user-generated content by Starbucks when customers competed in having their designs printed on their reusable plastic cups.

Remember to moderate all posts shared by the group and never allow any form of spam. Spot spammers and weed them out quickly if you intend to have a group where members have the best possible experience. Groups require a lot of commitment, so you will have to show up frequently to welcome new members and encourage discussions. As groups grow, engagements also decrease, which then requires that you segment the larger groups into smaller and more focused ones. Poor engagements can lead to the dismantling of a group with even tens of thousands of members.

Use Organic Post Targeting

Targeting is not only limited to ads, but you can also target your organic posts to ensure that you reach the right audience. For effective organic post targeting, you can engage in the following:

- Serve your post to the relevant customers based on age, gender, location, education and interest.
- Set an end date when the posts should stop showing up on their newsfeed
- Your post should target at least 20 people; however, the threshold may change if your page has a few thousand followers.

Below is a sample of a targeting feature:

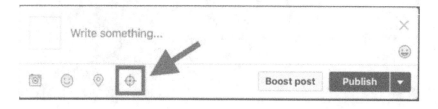

If it's not enabled, then you can target from the page settings. You can also restrict who gets to see your post. For better targeting, you can get Facebook Insights data for your audience and choose targeting parameters based on your business goals.

Once you have targeted the posts, you can then look into how they have performed. To know the type of content you should be creating, you can conduct a poll.

Publish Native Videos on Facebook

There has been a shift in video content over recent years with Facebook averaging over 8 billion video views each day. Videos have been featured as the strongest performers in newsfeeds. Native videos are in feed and are non-disruptive. These videos are specifically formatted for the social media platform that's hosting it, and they are not openly promotional. Native videos are more information based, engaging and highly targeted. They don't interfere with the user experience and tend to mimic other content available on the platform, capturing attention without any sound.

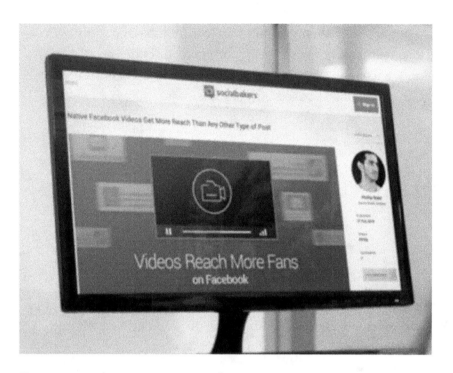

To get started posting native videos:

- You need to keep it short - like two minutes or even shorter.
- Make it look more professional; ensure that you use sufficient lighting and quality editing.
- Edit the video for a good thumbnail.
- You can also add a "call to action" if you want to engage further with viewers.

You can pin a featured video on your video section to attract more viewers. The featured video will appear prominently below the About section. You can embed your videos with blog posts as that may create a great multimedia experience for the blog audience. It may also increase engagement with your post on Facebook. As much as you can embed videos from YouTube, you can also choose to upload them directly onto the platform as Facebook favors native uploads over embedded videos. Native videos normally get a reach that's two times more with more "likes", shares and comments as compared to embedded ones.

Test Posting Frequency

When it comes to Facebook marketing, the quality of your content and its consistency are key factors that influence your social media success. Studies have shown that there are optimal posting frequencies that appeal differently to various social media groups. The posting frequency you use for Twitter should be different from that used for Facebook. If you fail to post frequently, then your audience may even forget that you exist while posting too frequently can make you a nuisance and it may dread seeing your posts overcrowd their newsfeed.

It's important to note that huge websites such as Huffington post, New York Times or Telegraph publish huge amounts of content daily and aggressively push their content on Facebook, so at times it may seem as if there is no limit to the posting frequency. The fact that big brands engage in such practices doesn't permit an average brand to follow suit; in fact it may prove to be unrealistic. Engagement tends to decrease when you engage in frequent posting. The rule of thumb is to keep between 1 – 3 posts per day.

When engaging in Facebook marketing, you should consider the following posting frequency:

- Avoid posing more than three times per day as it's likely to overwhelm your audience.
- If you have an international audience, you can post more often at different times. Such a move will help you reach diverse segments of followers in different time zone or those who get to log into Facebook occasionally.
- Remember to post high-quality content always. Add humor, educational content and inspiration to your posting.
- You can still be successful with a higher posting frequency as long as you provide great content. Mix your schedule for posting different types of content.
- Take time and test your page frequency. You can get insight on how your audience responds to your data.

According to Sprout social, below are some of the actions that many users find annoying:

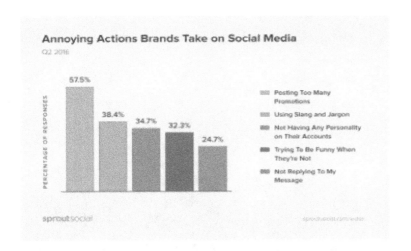

Partner with Other Facebook Pages Within Your Niche

Another way to enhance your organic reach is by partnering with authority brands within your niche. As much as one out of 10 business page owners may agree; it's a great way of benefiting from each other's audience. For example, you can offer to share their blog on your Facebook page while they do the same for you. You may both benefit from increased number of likes and clicks to your lead and sales pages.

You can take a look at some of the media websites such as Huffington post and Elite Daily, both of which have around 20 million Facebook fans; and the audience is similar for some of the content they publish. This is mostly because they share each other's blog posts on their Facebook pages. Such a strategy helps in boosting views for both parties and also provides them with quality content they haven't spent time creating. This is a smart media marketing strategy that if well implemented can lead to great results. This is an example of shared content from different pages.

They avoid the bandwagon.
(from The Huffington Post)

8 Habits Of Incredibly Interesting People
But what exactly makes them so captivating?
HUFFINGTONPOST.COM

If you are to realize great results from this strategy, you need to engage with pages that have ten thousands of likes, which also mean you need to have an influencer outreach strategy that's solid. Consider the following:

- Find out if your target influencer is right contextually. Your brand should resonate well with their audience. Promoting your brand to an audience that's misaligned may not yield the desired impact.

- You should also find out about the extent of their reach. Your influencer may not need millions of followers to engage with; they could just be in need a reach that's solid enough.

- Find out about the extent of their authority. Your influencer should have sufficient influence that can help inspire action amongst their audience.

- Consider your leverage. If you target a brand with a massive following and authority, then you should equally have something that's valuable and worth offering.

Engage in Brand Advocacy

One of the greatest strategies to generate buzz for your brand is turning your fans, employees and customers into brand advocates. Think of brands known for their loyal fans such as Apple, Nike and Microsoft. The fans are committed to promoting their products and content consistently without being paid any incentive. You can also develop an effective advocacy program for your brand. Below are some of the ideas you may to implement:

- Reach out and engage with the right people. You can begin with your employees as you cultivate a culture of advocacy.

- You can offer loyalty points and rewards to your customers. Consider giving referral bonuses to those who have recruited more people to the network.

- Consider developing topnotch customer service and become committed to providing value to customers.

- Create special content that your brand advocates can share in real time with their networks.

- Take time to measure the effectiveness of your program. You can do so by tracking sales from the referral links. You will see the level of engagement on branded content and the overall performance of brand advocates.

Make use of Your Email List

You can use your mailing list to inspire social actions. By including your Facebook share buttons in your email newsletters, your customers or those subscribed to your mailing list can then share them with their own Facebook audience; and that may lead to increased likes and more clicks on your website. You can also ask your email subscribers to join your Facebook group for exciting conversations.

Other ways to increase your organic reach include:

- Running Facebook contests. All you have to do is set a goal that's likely to impact the organic search reach. The goal you set should be specific and measurable such as growing a fan base, generating more leads or even increasing engagement. According to your goal, decide on the type of contest you intend to run and tailor the method of entry to match your goal. You should also determine the rules of entry by first checking out Facebook's guidelines for contests and noting the challenges involved. You should decide on how you intend to select the winner, the prize to be awarded and the promotion strategy.

- You can share on your Facebook profile posts from your page. To drive significant results, you will require at least

1,000 friends on your personal profile. This strategy helps in boosting post views. This marketing method is not scalable, so you just use it as one of your strategies and not the main one.

- Facebook is built to accommodate the use of hashtags, so consider using them; but try and limit yourself to only two per post. You should use hashtags correctly. You can make your hash tags unique to your brand so as not to be confused with others. You can use branded hashtags for tracking your brand equity on Facebook. You can also use hashtags as a way of navigating through your Facebook groups. Remember that a unique URL is created by Facebook for each hashtag used, which means that you can use hashtags to search for content. Remember to take advantage of trending topics and the corresponding hashtags.

- Use outstanding visual content. Avoid the use of grays and blues as they are dominant colors on Facebook and are more likely to morph into user's newsfeed. Use colors that will automatically be recognized such as red, orange and yellow.

- Create multiple visuals for each post. You can carry out an A/B test to see the post that performs well. After carrying out several tests, you will recognize a pattern which may show that the audience is more likely to respond to a given post better than another.

- Add call-to-action buttons on the image to enhance visual cues that influence users to click on the image. Instead of using stock photos, humanize your brand by using real human photos. You can capture attention through use of short captions of about 80 characters or less. Such a simple act can enhance engagement about 66%.

- You can ask questions when posting content to have higher engagement. You can also take advantage of the constant Facebook app updates. Make it your priority to stay informed with these updates and master them fast to tap into their capabilities for your benefit. Some of the updates you can take advantage of for maximum use include:

  o Facebook messenger bots. You can use them to engage with audience further.
  o 360 degree photos and videos; you can use them to capture a 360 degree panoramic view. Use it to capture group shots of workspaces and even events. It helps in expressing the human element of your brand.
  o Facebook offers can be used to create coupons and share promotional offers and discounts on your business page.
  o Intuitive and flexible videos: users don't have to tap on videos for them to play. It enables you to scroll through the newsfeed while still watching.

Chapter 5: Facebook Paid Marketing Strategy

An effective use of a social media marketing strategy requires a clear understanding of how one can leverage Facebook ads. With the vast number of posts every day, having your posts feature in your audience newsfeed regularly is continually becoming a challenge. Paid marketing makes it possible to reach your target audience with your content. Engaging in paid advertising without a proper understanding of how one can go about it may not bear much fruit. One thing that makes paid advertising quite effective is the fact that even those who are not targeted can still engage with the content, which then leads to enhanced organic reach as well.

Before you start engaging in paid marketing, there are questions you should ask yourself such as how effective is it? What type of engagement are you likely to get? What should you expect from your investment? Remember that you can either choose to boost your post or create an ad. Ads are normally created through the Ad Manager while boosted posts can be run through your Facebook page directly. You must publish a post on your page before deciding to boost it; however an ad runs independently.

To boost a post, all you have to do is to click on "boost post" at the bottom of your post. You can then select the objective you intend to achieve with the boosted post. Promoted posts are charged at a flat rate with the aim of reaching a given number of users.

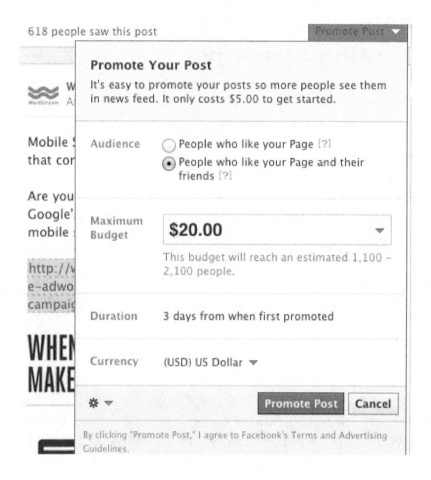

The fact that you have created a post is not a guarantee that it will appear on your followers' newsfeeds, so boosting a post helps increase its reach and may also enhance engagement with the post.

How to set up a Facebook ads Campaign

Before you begin creating your ads, it's vital that you first take time and think of the reason why you are advertising and what you intend to achieve from the action. You need to have a clear goal in place.

- Direct traffic from Facebook to your website
- Increase attendance for a given event
- Increase your Facebook content reach
- Generate new leads
- Increase engagement on your Facebook page

Once you have your goal for the campaign clear, you can begin the setup process. Facebook ad campaigns are generally done through the Facebook ads manager tool and can be directly accessed through facebook.com/ads or by clicking on Manage Ads in your Facebook's drop down menu. You can create your ad by using Power Editor or Ads Manager.

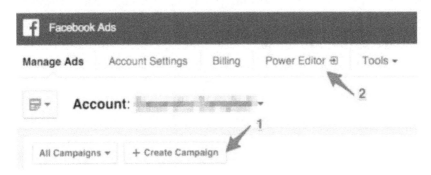

Choose Marketing Objective

Facebook offers a number of objectives based on what you intend to accomplish with your advert. For each of these objectives, you can choose from various formats based on your marketing goal and target audience. Begin by choosing your marketing objective for the campaign you intend to create. Below are some of the marketing objectives from which you can choose:

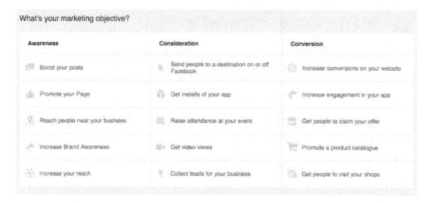

With a small budget of $1 dollar per day, you can reach a good audience; however as you design your campaign, consider going for objectives with the potential of impacting your bottom line, such as those below.

- Direct people to a destination within Facebook or to your website with the intention of increasing website conversions
- Get more people to download your app to increase engagement with your app
- Increase attendance to your event and get people into claiming your offer, or get people to visit your shop
- Get views for your video
- Collect business leads

Once you have selected the marketing objective, you can then go ahead and give your campaign a name.

Define Target Audience and Budget

This is a very crucial step having the potential of influencing your success with Facebook marketing. You can either create a custom audience, which may include reaching people who have already interacted with your business, or you can also create a similar audience to one you have already interacted with. Or you can go for an audience you used in a previous campaign. You can select your target audience based on the following factors:

Location: Begin with country, then state, city, zip code or address; you can still refine further as desired. Age, gender, languages, interests, behaviors and connections

Targeting & Placement ✎ Edit

Location:
United States

Interests: Social media

Excluded Connections:
Pages
Exclude people who like Buffer

Age: 18 - 65+

Language: English (US)

Mobile Placement: News Feed

Desktop: News Feed or Right Column

Estimated Daily Reach

1,200 - 3,200 people

0   of 14,000,000 ⓘ

This is only an estimate. Numbers shown are based on the average performance of ads targeted to your selected audience.

Setting Your Budget

Once you have selected your target audience, then go ahead and choose the amount you want to spend on the campaign. The figure you choose generally represents the maximum amount you intend to spend. You can then set your budget to daily or lifetime. A daily budget is the amount you will spend each day while a lifetime budget is the total amount you intend to spend over the campaign period.

Budget & schedule
Define how much you'd like to spend, and when you'd like your adverts to appear. Learn more.

Budget ⓘ | Daily budget ▾ | £11.00
£11.00 GBP

Actual amount spent per day may vary. ⓘ

Schedule ⓘ | ○ Run my advert set continuously starting today
⦿ Set a start and end date

| Start | 📅 9/1/2017 | 🕐 08:40 |
| End | 📅 9/2/2017 | 🕐 08:40 |
(London Time)

Your adverts will run for **31 days**. You'll spend no more than **£341.00**.

Show advanced options ▾

Create your Advert

Creating an advert requires a lot of work as it's at this stage when you choose the appropriate headline, the body text, and where the ad will be displayed on Facebook. You can either create your ad using an existing post or by creating a new advert. Begin by selecting the format you intend to use for the advert. Facebook ads generally look different depending on the type of results you intend to get, and you can choose from five options.

- Carousel: enables you to create an ad with scrollable videos or images
- Single image: enables you to create up to six variations of your ad by using one image
- Single video: enables you to create an advert using one video
- Slide show: enables you to create a looping video using up to ten images
- Canvas: enables you to share an immersive story by combining videos with images

Remember that the format you choose will be influenced by the objective of your advert. Once you have selected the format, go ahead and add content. If your advert is to be a success, put more emphasis on the image and the content as they should be enticing enough for people to click. The recommended specifications are normally shown next to the area where you are to upload your content. The recommended image size is 1200 x 628 pixels, image ration is 1.91.1; and to maximize delivery of your advert, consider using an image that doesn't have an overlaid text or very little.

For video specs, the format should be either MOV or MP4 files, resolution of at least 720p, full size of 2.3 GB maximum, ration 16:9, and Facebook time 60 minutes maximum.

Place Your Order

Once you are through with all these steps, the next thing to do is to place your order. You can then go ahead and submit your order which will be reviewed by Facebook before it goes live. You will be notified through an email once the advert is live. A budget of $5 per day is more likely to give you 10 likes per day, 1 click to your landing page and about 800 people reached with your boosted post.

To effectively run paid promotions, consider installing a Facebook tracing pixel on your website. A Facebook pixel enables you to track actions undertaken on your website and other landing pages. It also allows you to build custom audiences that enable you to retarget the people who have visited your website. For example, let's say that you searched for a given product from a website, but you left without making a purchase after clicking. You may realize that wherever you go, you are followed with ads about the same product: those are retargeted ads.

A pixel was placed on your device when you visited the website, and they can therefore send you follow up messages with the intention of influencing you to come back and make a purchase. With a pixel installed, you can see the people who visited your website and can then send them ads related to the products they saw there. You can start by reaching out to them with a blog post to get their attention. To have effective paid marketing, consider engaging in the following for greater results:

Awareness

Before you create an advert, you need to first capture people's attention by creating awareness about your products and services. Give priority to creating awesome content that your audience will consider valuable and helpful. Your content should help them solve some of the problems they may be having and also make them laugh. Once you have created that awareness through your Facebook page, then you can pull them to your website. You should not just focus on getting website traffic; you need traffic that will help you create a new custom audience.

You will find a custom audience by identifying their interests such as the brands and the people they follow. Once you identify this, go ahead and refine the demographics such as location, gender, age and the like.

Consideration

Since the first campaign was focused on creating awareness, you can now capitalize on the engagement created by sending offers to these people. They should be transformed from prospects to leads. Your ads should be tailored to those who have already visited your website and are aware of the products you offer. You should therefore focus on getting information from them while spending the least amount of money; you can do this through a lead magnet where you can send them something like an invitation to a webinar, an eBook or even a checklist. This should be done in exchange for their email.

Your audience targeting at this stage is much easier, as you will be sending ads to those with some information about your website and products. If your site is a big one, then you can limit the audience to 30 or 60 days to ensure you're reaching those most engaged who have fresh memories of your brand. The right offer has the potential of capturing their attention.

Conversions

Once you have engaged in all the hard work by building up the necessary attention and generating leads, the last step is to send product offers, those that seem too good to be true, so they hand over their payment information. If your products are high priced, then you can consider reducing the price for your Facebook audience. Now that you are well equipped with a strategy, you can work towards implementing it effectively so that you can convert strangers to loyal customers.

How to Create a Realistic Budget for Your Paid Marketing

Knowing the right budget to spend if you have never carried out Facebook marketing before can be a challenge. To find out about a tentative budget, ask yourself the following questions; how much your product or service is, the number you intend to sell and your present conversion rate. For example, assume that your product value is $100 and you intend to sell 10 of them with your current conversion rate at 1%.

You now do some math to figure it out. If you are to make $1,000 out of 10 sales with a conversion rate of 1%, then you may require 1000 visits or clicks from your ad. So you need to figure out how much 1000 clicks will cost so that you know the amount to set aside for your daily ad budget. Your objective should be clear like link clicks or conversions so that Facebook can help you realize the goal.

Sponsored Stories

You can also enhance your market space through use of sponsored stories as they enhance interactions with your Facebook audience. Sponsored stories work like word of mouth marketing. A user is more likely to pay keen attention to a page when they notice that some of their friends have "liked" the page. The main goal of sponsored stories is to influence a user to take the same action as their friends. If a business wants more likes, then friends who have liked the page will be shown. If that business wants more offers, then friends who have claimed the offer will be found. Below is an example of a sponsored story.

Sponsored stories don't only apply to offers and likes; they can be used with Facebook open graph apps of any kind. According to Facebook, sponsored stories contribute to higher CTRs by 46%, which makes them a great Facebook marketing strategy. Sponsored stories can also be created easily by going to Facebook ad create flow.

Even as you engage in paid marketing, you should always focus on being cost effective and relevant. Try to stay within your budget to avoid getting clicks that may not add value. Ad expenses can really shoot up when you don't have a clear target group. As much as targeting a large group can be great for creating awareness, relevance is very critical when doing Facebook ads. Try to reach out more to customers and custom audiences that fit your brand well. Your content should therefore communicate some sense of identity by showcasing your brand effectively such as in your logo and the way the business colors are displayed.

Your content should have some type of reward which may be in the form of an offer code, an industry guide, a whitepaper, a deal or promotion. The tone of the content should be the same across the entire Facebook page and website as well. Finally, your content should incorporate some element of action. Include a call to action that's clear and precise in line with your Facebook goals.

Conclusion

Congratulations and thank you for taking the time to download this **Facebook Marketing** book. Whether you have engaged in Facebook marketing before or are just starting out, I know the information shared in this book has shed more light on areas that you can begin working on. Just as there is such a large pool of potential customers on Facebook, there are equally numerous businesses and competitors out there trying their best to get the customers attention and who have the upper hand business wise. So implementing my marketing strategies effectively has the potential of giving you an edge over the competition.

It's vital that you take every step seriously and to implement the strategy of choice even as you still take time to understand the platform better. The only way you can fully grasp some of the strategies shared here is by trying them out; you will see that they can save you a lot of time and may also lead to tangible business growth. Just like in any other business, realizing your desired outcome may not be possible if you don't have clear goals and objectives in place. Your goals should be beyond getting "likes" and clicks; it should be related to engaging in strategies likely to yield the desired conversion.

If you find an area that's not very clear, take your time and go through it again for more clarity so implementation becomes much easier. There are numerous small businesses that have grown into big brands just by understanding the dynamics of Facebook marketing and investing time to monitor and evaluate what works and what doesn't. There are strategies that worked a few years ago but may not deliver the same results given the continuous tweaking of the application and algorithms. As a business owner, you will have to be flexible and more willing to flow with the changes as they come if you are to realize sustained business growth through the platform.

Thank you for buying this book; however, I have one request - would you kindly leave a review for the book? It'd be greatly appreciated.

Thank you and wishing you well in your business!